An antholog

G000241341

Fall in love
with Love with me?

Rachna Chowla

For all those forever swirling leaves that bless my
being, and the poems that visit

Universal questions?

If you were the planet Jupiter
  I would be one of your rings
        Or perhaps
        All of sixty-seven of your moons
    And if you were a comet
    Blazing with your quiet radiance
    Across the heavens
        I would be your tail

  But, you happen to be my Universe
    So, where exactly does that leave me?

Longing and parachutes

Here I am
Counting infinity
Dividing the indivisible
Being present in some future
That is yet to come by

All because
You decided
To drop
Into my thoughts today
A parachute falling

Blown by the winds of destiny
Being called by the light
That lives inside me
Only
Because
You exist.

Eyes of truth

I bask in eternity, every cell soaked
With You, with truth
With every kiss ever kissed
And every loving embrace too
When just the thought of You
Skips through my mind
Carefree like a bird
Flit-fluttering
Across the skies

Imagine what a glance might do?

Nightfall

Shadowed light
Painted
With dusky rays
And a blurry hum

Every colour, and none
Ablaze

Awake, settling ever so
As the undulating clouds in my breath
Wispily fold me
Into
The edges of sight
Just long enough for time to linger
And for Us, to meet

How delightful, those still gazes from the stars
That live inside your eyes...

Shades of You

Colours translucent, matted luminescence
Lush strokes forging unseen winds
A thousand skies hanging
In the invisibility of the stars

And every quantum, that sings Your name.

Enhaloed by time

The curves of time
Have their own idea
Their own flows
But sometimes

In truth, more often than not

How I wish
They would allow me
To draw them into a circle

And place us perfectly in the middle

Or perhaps they have
And I just didn't notice?

My wanderlust

How I longed to roam
Walk along rivers
Feet wet in the ocean's calling
That flows between lands

Not known to me, but longed for
And all in some attempt to know You

But, then, in that moment when we met
And I fell inside those eyes azure

My wanderlust, wandered off

What need to roam to the ends of the Earth?
When knowing Your Love
We travel beyond everywhere
Without ever leaving here.

Constancy

Spectral blues as free as the sky
Undulating, unaccountably dilating
A drop
Of ink, perfect, round

The door to the Moon

Wide, wild with serenity
And the constancy
Of Your Love for Me

How could I even ask for one more breath?

What is this alchemy?

This You
  That merges
          With this Me?
        Covalency
   Where this We
  Dissolves
   And touch, soluble, unfelt
Disperses
   Like breath
   Absorbed by the pores of existence
Birthed into its rivers
   Delivering all there is
      Into its ocean of alchemy.

Ripples of Us

Us, in the middle of that pond
Wearing only each other
Under the cover of the quivering evening light
As it cascades playfully through the leaves

You, holding me still
And me, holding you
Us, among the reflections of the passing clouds
And a raindrop, or two

So close, that our breaths rise and fall
In harmony
With our beating hearts
Together

As we merge with the gentle
Undulations
Of this watery universe
Where every whispering ripple
Speaks only of Love.

Eyes like treacle

Molten amber, rich of Earth and Moon
Unhurried in their unfolding
Stretching, unrolling
With a treacle sweet slowness
Of space
Captivated between breaths
Where time rests, suspended
And the glassy lake of quiet beauty
Remains not as a mirror
But becomes

With Us too, the door.

La découverte

A pleasant pause
    Weightless with Summer

Stairs taken, silence met
  Held, holding
    Melded, moulding

La découverte
    Ever-deepening meaning

Languages lost
  Rhythms found
  Floating, Us
    As a sea of beauty filled weightlessness.

Dance of the iris

Sight, muted, eclipsed
By a collapse of everything
Into a pulse

Blue to blue
And back
Dilating ever so
A dance of the iris

And breath in time
With a metronome
That knows no place
Nor time

And Us, lying in between
The lines of a stave
As instruments, porous to the music
That pervades and embraces
Us back to life.

The come-hither of the cosmos

A thousand thousand grains of sand
Crystalled soft in ebb and flow
As endings unfold, like waves
Before their own beginnings
And my being too, as them
Hovering
Translucently so
As a thousand thousand eyes look through me
And I, look through them
But a conduit
Between the seas in the skies
And the skies in the seas
And all that shines forth
As the come-hither of the cosmos.

Surrender

Moments meant not for meaning
Just moments dancing in being

Unravelled yet entangled

An eternal circularity in the straight lines

Of Love

Sparkling with unknowing
A coalescence
Distilled always

Into a drop of You
No matter what.

Set your sails towards yearning

I know the winds seem strong and harsh
And often sweep us away

But my sweet

Set your sails towards yearning
And let your mind ask why
But don't let it answer

Just let your heart's compass be your guide
And I shall wait for your there
Beyond yearning's yearning for itself.

My mantra

Soak me in your silence
Undress me of form?
Come, let us swim again
And float
Gazing towards the stars

Where each twinkle spells out your name
Over and over and over again

Will you be my mantra too?

Your under-study for my searching eyes

I love those days
　　When I know you will come by
　I love the anticipation
　　But know how it will be
　　How it always is
　　　　　Lovely
　　How I can't help but wrap myself around you
　　　And you just can't resist
　Like a petal of a rose
Inside another, inside another, inside another

　　And those long moonbeam glances
　　　That pop up from our pockets
　　Telling of stories from other lifetimes
　　　And of other lifetimes
　　　　With the faintest of smiles
　　　Your pupils dilate just a touch

　　And there I am
　　　　　Swimming
　　In that very instant
　　　And you too
　　And even on the days when we can't swim
　　　There is always the Moon
　Up there in the sky
　Your under-study
　　　For my searching eyes.

No more hide and seek?

Find me
There, always hiding
In the moments
Of not noticing, and of noticing
And the betweeness that hides between
Unnoticed
Except by you
Where just the never distant memory
Of my eyes brings a songful silence
A bathing of fragrance
To your soul
And the knowing
That because we met
And meet in this moment
We meet in every moment

So my Love, no more hide and seek?

Expectations...

Walk with me
Across to the edge of the horizon
And hold me, as we hop across to the Moon?

As we leave behind all the hum drum
And dance by the sea of tranquillity
As passing comets sing us a tune?

And perhaps a dip too, a little swim?
Gazing up at the Earth as it floats with the stars
A blue hue, a blue kohl line around the sky's eye

I know I ask too much, so just one last request
Spin my thoughts too my Love, like the Earth
Spun into revolution, who knows why?

Let the asking and yearning find a home
In me and in some faraway galaxy and make
Thunderous new stars and spells of quanta of light

Where they might still appear as the tide's song
When we meet in the centre of the all this noise
As we dance on the Moon as you hold me tight?

Borromean rings

Echoes
    Of silence
        Smudging my edges
   Bevels rounding
   Horizons lost
Stillness rippling
       Oscillations in a field

Of Beautiful Borromean rings

    Mirroring Your eternal symmetry
  In Your eternity
    Where
  We too are lost
    And found
  In All.

My ghazal

The language of love
       Resting, on once enlivened leaves
   They too made of song
       Leaves drifting, but not in a storm
   Inked edges dispersing into the white

Letters lifting from a page

       Taking flight on semaphore of waves
   Soaked with the love of ancient tales
           Finding solace again through the doors

Of Your Eyes

   And light again in Your words
       Each laced with Your love-soaked soul
       Winged by clouds, free with their dreams
   And composed into existence
   Just to whisper
           'That You are my ghazal
   My language of Love'.

Both mirror and glass

Your eyes are like both mirror and glass
And there, in their capacious hold
I find Me with You, reflected in our own infinity

That finds itself, back through the looking glass
In my eyes, as they gaze back into Yours
And as Your eyes, like both mirror and glass
Capacious in their hold

Show You with Me, reflected in our own infinity
That finds us, reflections of one another
Back and forth, forth and back
Until
There is nothing to reflect.

The sea of eudaimonia

Glassy waters still as light
Whisper
Of that amniotic silence
That once bathed my being
And now, Your light gilded
Feather soft, glides
Swathing me, taking me
Wallowing me into wonder
Cosmic jazz in every deliquescent touch
Each atom distilled of logic
Charged again
A conduit to the sea of eudaimonia
Where we meet, to skate
In Our synchronicity
Naked
Of form.

She is the ocean's plume

When she walks
   Along the shore, feet bare
      Sinking into the minerals beneath
     Soaking up the wisdom of the sea
  The waves listen to her stories
    And soothe them with their slow sway
    Tickling her soles as they do
   With the twinkle of faraway stars

  Reminding her to let her thoughts
     Fall away, with each wave's sway

   So that the gentle swell that dwells deep
  And glides with the elegance of a swan
   Can swathe her with the ocean's foamy plume

    And call her back to herself.

You are that last sliver of light

You are that last sliver of light
A wide azure that surrenders to its dreams
The lingering perfume of a sweet rose
That suffuses my everyday with its gentle touch
The feeling of being held, by You
That has soaked into my every cell
All from a moment's moment
Filled with Us
Floating, eyes closed suspended in time
Hearts opened seeing between the cracks

The tick-tock workings of the cosmos
Breathing, beating, billowing, being
Being, billowing, beating, breathing
In their own not-so tick-tock way
Painting all into existence
And Us
As we stare at ourselves
Staring at ourselves
And at Our vanishing
Into that last sliver of silvery light.

Serendipity was a Summer's day

Serendipity was a Summer's day
Fresh, airy, filled with the glisten of the sun
Hopping across the leaves
And the relief of something
Filling my senses

And two otherwise parallel lines
On a quest for eternity

Being brought into focus
Not two lines were they ever
But one

Cross-sectionally
Nothing more than a tiny dot
So momentary
In the vastness of existence

But containing all of existence itself
And the serendipity of space and time
But mostly, the serendipity
That was that Summer's day

Which has made every day since
No matter what the season
An exquisite Summer's day.

Threads, loose

That day of Summer
Lines lost themselves to themselves
  Blurred without verges

Smooth, with a language of coherence
  Unnoticed until
The clouds softness folded
Into the freedom of the trees
  And your eyes, argent and unshy

That already understood

Fell with mine through the watery mirror
As the way appeared to meet us
And my contoured breath too, yielded
        Finally, to yours
The reversal of education
A corridor where we walk
Binocular, in waves, a double helix seen
An illusion of the clock only to see double
As we have both come to know of certitude
  Our well-travelled companion

Who carries us still
  Through pastures new
Due north, pointing always to Us.

Enraptured conversation

I know what you left unsaid
It was felt, words unneeded
And I too wanted to say, to write back
And I did
With the stars
That floated in their stillness
And the sky too, with its enveloping hold
That held the patterns made by the rain
On the window, as you watched
The world slide into pastel clear lines
As waves of the Earth rotated towards you
Then vanished, washed away into the past

Drops of heaven, drops of me
Dropping by to say

Me too...

The synchronicity of silence

How so, like moonlight
Do your eyes
Seduce mine
Undressing my iris
With waves inside
That throw open

The door to my soul?

Something in You
Speaks directly with something in me
It must be the synchronicity of silence

Where, I am always the last to know...

The Goddess Venus

Lines
Travelling at the speed of light
As the last pixel of ebony
Fades into a hanging sea azure
Scintillating still
With the not knowing
That makes me feel
Lost
And found
Both
In the same moment

But it was fading into the sea
That allowed the Goddess Venus to emerge…

.

Slip-sliding

If the search continues, could it be
That I am the search?

So there can't be any going
Even to the stars
Even of the stars

Where their travelling apart
Makes them stay, just as they are
Or move closer still

Leaving the sky, empty of space but filled
With the sparkle of organza
Where too the darkness appears

Just in a blink

With the light of the stars too, on the other side

So I shall sit and wait
To start and to end, and to slip-slide between
And to not be too lost
Searching for that, which has already found me.

Cherry blossom moons

Bark, browned bare
By the bones of winter
Almost banished behind its own back
Husked rice, but rice no less

Resting

Inside the bliss of a frosted hull
Waiting, what waits for it

The awakening of Spring
And the season
Of cherry blossom moons.

Your hush

A crowd blurred
Into pulsed passages
           Phased, paused, free

    Concentric, I wait

    Inside the anticipation of your hush
Steps away, you
        Less steps, You

  Space between, forgotten
        Steps between, lost

   We fold in
  Under the covers
    Of a balmy evening sky
    And wander
   Through answers, before questions
  Endings before beginnings

 And the Us before there was ever
  A You or an I.

Symphony

Horizons, edges, illusions of the eye
What need for journeys?
When far and near
Reside in the merging of all clocks
And their forgetting

Which is no forgetting at all

But living, awaking not dreaming
In the space between the music
That gives its symphony
And the moment's welcoming to nothing
But itself.

Monsoon rains and Us

Walking, Always

Even when I am still
I am walking to You

And like the Monsoon rains
And a dry Indian Summer

We meet

Before carrying on, on our way
Towards each other again

But not alone

For I carry You
And You carry Me
In the perpetuity of motion
Walking our own orbits, yet still

Together, at the nexus of Us.

The door

I know we live in impossibility
But that star up there
That we both see

It isn't a star
It's a door

Where words cannot enter
Nor those comfy-have-me-holds

Even kisses must be left outside
Only space and silence can slip through

Meet me on the other side?

The breath of quiescence

One hand mine, the other yours
Let me fold myself inside your breath

And escape

The way a gentle neap tide escapes its physique
Unravelling itself, into itself
Fusing, diffusing
Deliquescing, liquescing
Merging, melding
Beyond a honeyed subtlety
Unlaced

Wandering, euphonious in its quiescence
Where it just is
Like me, when I am with You

And where we, with quiescence itself
Dissolve into its breath.

Imprints ethereal

Shadows
   A confluence of matter
Waves of invisibility

Clipped, held by the appearance
Of form, any and all

  Disciplined lines
Leaving imprints of each torso
  Upon this slated surface

That moves
   With laissez-faire sway
Of waves playing, beside Jupiter's full moons

Imprints ethereal, us, on this Earth?
  Or perhaps, words important
In the conversations of the Universe?

Ferrous meetings

Dense pigments
  Both shades of light
 Isomers, though fixed

Ferrous, they met

    To be caught
      By the irresistible cadence of life

   And watch the improviso
 Shifting, shaping
   Tectonic shivers
All
   Invisible bridges to their souls
And
Thankfully
   With no end in sight.

A delicious addiction

A delicious addiction
I have to You
And whilst you stay
On the other side of the hills
I somehow remain with You
Inside this forever full Moon
Alight with an ember
Of warm sweetness

From those eyes

That sing without words
A song sung only for me
Of our tender caressed moments
That belong to a dream
Spent in your arms

And when I wake
Small crumbs I find

A trail, walked with eyes shut
That I know will lead me
Back to Us.

Majesty

Eyes closed by the appearance of the stars
  Majestic, they call
Amnesic, of I don't know what
 I lay
  Yet like mists
   They drift in my dreams
    Some nights clear and bright
     Enough to waken the morning Sun
    Other nights thick with fog
  Amnesic of themselves

But what always hangs in their filament
   And in the moments
  Before I surrender to my dusk
And to my dawn
  And the moments in between

        Is You.

A glimpse

Words winged appear
   In the white spaces of love and possibility
Etched like water in water
         Into the ashened fading
   Of a fading moment of wanting
And the wanting them, to rearrange

Then, a glimpse of balance

  A leaf swirling, free
And just as she falls
  As and where she is meant

 The evaporation, of the seeming precision
Of a moment yet to be
  And relief, and breath stretching to all horizons

  Pupils dilating, revealing an optic assemblage
That has always been
  Of holding, and being held close
A tender caress
    As I uncling
     From the membrane of myself
  And fall, with her
Into your arms
   Wherever You are.

Are you close?

Surging, pulsating

Not me, You
Here, not here
My heart, breathless
Vibrations effortless

Rippling the silence

That dissipates all noise
Even my voice asking,
'Are you
Close?'
And you answered my question
Before it appeared

How time somersaults back over itself
To allow us to meet, again and again?

Drifting the light

Like liquid they are, flowers
Those thready-floured yellow sprigs
Hiding among the beginnings
Of the tender, silkened petals
That sometimes sway
And at other times sink into their own fluency

But always
Drift the light with the shadow
Allowing their fragrance to waft

Another poem, taking flight...

Into our dance

My eyes hidden under the waves
Of my hair, that play
In your close breath
As you whisper...

'I just wanted to tell you
That when you wear that dress
And whirl in your dance
I see my Love turning into a flower
A hibiscus I think
And like a moth, I am caught
Bewitched
Watching a flame
My flowery flame
And as I watch further
I cannot tell
Whether you exist outside of me
Or whether this world exists outside of Us
And then
When I surrender

It all just merges
Into Our dance'

The knowings of Venus

Mysterious
> From the very start
A little curious too
> With a sparkle
Self-evident

Seen last when gazing at Venus
Nuzzled under a winter eve's Moon

Yet here he was
Wearing it
As if Venus had borrowed it from him

And when that ocean of warmth poured forth
From his eyes
Travelling through each atom
That stood mesmerised between us
And reached the shores of my soul

I too knew what He and Venus
Have always known…

Venus

Parallel lines
Spinning with a slowing ease
And a geometric knowing
Of nowhere, but that place of all beauty
Waiting inside each moment's floating Moon

An invitation to fall
Into an ever reposing sea
A dance, under its watery edge
That plays itself, the plainsongs of our Venus

And there, as ever the intertwined odyssey
Of falling away
Each time unfolding
An unfolding, and another, until
Every gravitational pull, grows ever slow
Grows ever still

And the moments between moon times
Fall too for the watery sea
Filled with dance
And a luminescence
In the geometry of shapes
That can't help but shift
Towards the slow rhythms
Of what gives each moment
Its own magnetic moment of Venus.

Buttoned stars

A button undone
In the canvas of stars
Unnoticed
Even by us

Allowing, rains of a mid-distance hush
Faint at first

And this is how we met [again]

Umbrellas forgotten
Overcoats lost
And happily soaked and sodden

Each droplet, a little note
Of guidance
In this rhythmic sonance

We call life

And for each little note
A star of thanks
I have learnt to plant
In that sky
That we always share.

This Utopian Chance

She doesn't know, but the sky drapes itself around
her like a sari and the stars yearn to hang from her
ears

The winds long to sail adrift in her breath, and the
monsoon rains to taste her sweetened tears

The sands of the Thar continually ask her for her
glow, but she hasn't yet learned to hear their prayer

And what of the liquid sparkle of the Sun that
tickles the ocean's waves? It wants nothing but to
caress her hair

The red petals of every rose want to be crushed
into a powder, just to sit close to her by pretending
to be sindhoor

And every bell in every temple awaits to be struck
when her heart beats, to feel her rhythm, such is
her unbeknownst-to-her allure…

The oceans too that stretch from one lifetime to the next, condense themselves into a single drop, waiting from her just one kiss

But she doesn't know, for her heart is clouded with clouds and thoughts of an illusory past amiss

If only she knew that the Moon wakes early every night, to bring her a message from that hidden stellate Sun

But she doesn't know, for her eyes are still covered by a mask, a mask of desires after which her tides still run

And then what of the emeralds of Aurora, the circus of lights skating across the skies, asking for her hand to dance

But she doesn't know, for her ears don't hear the music, even though for her it is sung. Oh, how long will she let slip this utopian chance?

Printed in Great Britain
by Amazon